KT-584-262

PRECIOUS EARTH

Energy Crisis

Jen Green

Chrysalis Children's Books

First published in the UK in 2003 by
Chrysalis Children's Books
An imprint of Chrysalis Books Group Plc
The Chrysalis Building, Bramley Road,
London W10 6SP

Copyright © Chrysalis Books Group Plc 2003

All rights reserved. No part of this book may be
reproduced or utilised in any form or by any means,
electronic or mechanical, including photocopying,
recording or by any information storage and retrieval
system, without permission in writing from the
publisher, except by a reviewer who may quote
brief passages in a review.

ISBN 1 84138 714 2

British Library Cataloguing in Publication Data for this
book is available from the British Library.

Editorial Manager: Joyce Bentley
Picture Researcher: Terry Forshaw
Produced by Tall Tree Ltd
Designer: Ed Simkins
Editor: Kate Phelps
Consultant: Michael Rand

Printed in China

Some of the more unfamiliar words used in this book
are explained in the glossary on page 31.

Photo Credits:
Front cover(main), Fred Dott/Still Pictures; front
cover(clockwise from top left), Ray Robert/Ecoscene;
Paul Gipe/Still Pictures; Larry Lee Photography/Corbis;
Angela Hampton/Ecoscene; 1, Reinhard Janke/Still
Pictures; 2, Science Museum, London/HIP; 4, Mark
Edwards/Still Pictures; 5(t), Paul Gipe/Still Pictures;
5(b), Franklin Hollander/Still Pictures; 6, Christine
Osborne/Ecoscene; 7(t), D. Hall/FLPA; 7(b), Jorgen
Schytte/Still Pictures; 8, Chrysalis Images; 9(t), Chris
Gill/Ecoscene; 9(b), Arnaud Greth/Still Pictures; 10,
Chinch Gryniewicz/Ecoscene; 11(t), Ray Pfortner/Still
Pictures; 11(b), Paul Glendell/Still Pictures; 12, Guido
Alberto Rossi/Getty Images; 13(t), Larry Lee
Photography/Corbis; 13(b), Andre Maslennikov/Still
Pictures; 14, David Vance/Getty Images; 15(t), Mark
Edwards/Still Pictures; 15(b), Brooklyn
Productions/Getty Images; 16, Marek Libersky/Still
Pictures; 17(t), Reinhard Janke/Still Pictures; 17(b), Sipa
Press/Rex Features; 18, Anthony Cooper/Ecoscene;
19, Christine Osborne/Ecoscene; 20, Andrew
Brown/Ecoscene; 21(t), Michael Coupard/Still Pictures;
21(b), Angela Hampton/Ecoscene; 22, Arnaud
Greth/Still Pictures; 23(t), Mark Edwards/Still Pictures;
23(b), Angela Hampton/Bubbles; 24, UN Photo
Library; 25(t), Science Museum, London/HIP; 25(b),
Thomas Raupach/Still Pictures; 26, Angela
Hampton/Ecoscene; 27(t), Julia Baine/Still Pictures;
27(b), Yellow Dog Productions/Getty Images; 28,
Angela Hampton/Bubbles; 29, Ray Robert/Ecoscene;
30, Mark Edwards/Still Pictures; 31, Larry Lee
Photography/Corbis; back cover, Arnaud Greth/Still
Pictures.

Contents

What is energy?

Energy is the mysterious force that makes things work. There are many different forms of energy. Most of the energy we use in our daily lives comes from machines that are powered by sources of energy called fuels.

Energy is the force that lights and heats our homes and schools. Machines such as cookers, fridges and computers use energy. Cars, buses and trains run on fuels that contain energy. Energy is essential to our lives. It is so convenient and easy to use that many people waste it. But fuel supplies such as coal, oil and gas are not endless – one day, they will run out.

▼ Fuels such as coal, oil and gas are burned in power stations to produce energy.

These wind turbines use the energy of the wind to make electricity without polluting the air.

Today the world faces an energy crisis because fuels are becoming scarce. There is also the problem of pollution, which is caused when fuels such as coal and oil are burned to produce energy. Scientists and governments are working to develop new, cleaner ways of producing energy. Everyone can help to ease the energy crisis and the problem of pollution by not wasting energy.

CLOSE TO HOME

Homes in rich countries use huge amounts of energy running machines, such as televisions, videos, cookers, washing machines and computers, and keeping rooms at a comfortable temperature. Look around your home and make a list of all the machines you can find that use energy.

Energy and fuel

Energy comes from many different sources. Plants get energy from sunlight. Animals and people get energy from their food. Machines run on electricity made by burning fuels such as coal, oil and gas. However, the mining and burning of these fuels creates problems for the natural world.

Energy can be changed from one form to another. When you strike a match, the wood burns, releasing energy in the form of light and heat. Electricity is a form of energy that is very convenient to use. It is supplied to our homes so we can use it any time we like, by just flicking a switch.

▼ In hot places, such as the Sahel region in Africa, cutting down too many trees has changed farmland into barren desert.

In some parts of the world, cutting down trees for firewood has created problems. Tree roots running underground help to hold the soil together. When too many trees are cut down, the soil becomes loose and then washes away after heavy rain. On this hillside, terraces have been built to try to prevent this.

◀ *A girl from Nepal in southern Asia carries a heavy load of firewood home for her family. Around half of all the people in the world still rely on wood for fuel.*

Wood was the first fuel used by humans. For thousands of years, people have burned wood to provide heat to keep warm and cook their food. In poorer countries, firewood is still the main source of energy, but in some areas wood is now becoming scarce.

Fossil fuels

Coal, oil and gas are the fuels most commonly used in rich countries. They are known as fossil fuels because they are the fossilised remains of plants and animals that lived millions of years ago but now lie buried underground.

The coal that burns brightly in some homes is actually the remains of tall, tree-like plants that grew in forests millions of years ago. When the trees died, they fell and later became squashed under new layers of vegetation. The squashed layers very slowly turned into coal.

▼ *During the eighteenth and nineteenth centuries, people discovered that coal could be burned to make energy for industry.*

Oil and gas are the remains of sea animals and plants that lived millions of years ago. When they died, their remains settled on the sea bed and were buried under new layers of sand or mud. Gradually they turned into black, sticky oil or pockets of natural gas. Oil and gas are often found together. They are mined on land and also out at sea from massive platforms called oil rigs.

Oil is the most important fuel used today. In factories called refineries, shown here, crude oil is processed to make fuels, including petrol and diesel, to run different vehicles. Many other useful products, including plastics, paint and nylon fabric, are also made from oil.

▶ Oil rigs that drill for undersea oil are huge, often the size of whole villages.

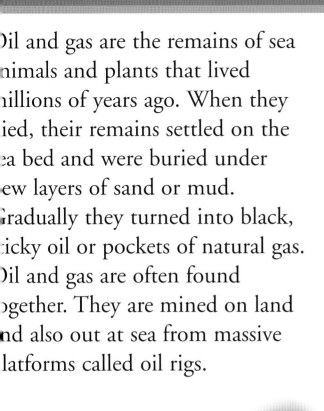

Using fossil fuels

Coal, oil and gas are the main fuels used to make life comfortable in rich countries. But when they are mined, transported and burned, these fuels can harm the natural world in several different ways.

On land, coal mines and oil wells spoil the landscape, and mines leave towering waste heaps. Mining also creates pollution, which poisons the air, the soil and local rivers and streams. Once mined, the fuel usually has to be carried over long distances to power stations, some of which are close to towns and cities. Transporting the fuel by truck, ship or pipeline may also pollute the environment if any fuels leaks out.

▲ Coal is often mined by boring a network of deep shafts and underground tunnels of mines like this one in Wales, Great Britain.

Fumes from factories and cars cause a haze of pollution called smog, which hangs above modern cities, like New York, shown here. People, particularly children, can develop breathing difficulties such as asthma and other health problems after breathing in this polluted air.

In 1996, the oil tanker Sea Empress *leaked rude oil into the sea after it was holed off the* Velsh coast. Local beaches were polluted, and thousands of seabirds died after their feathers were covered with oil.

Coal, oil and gas are burned at power stations to make steam that runs machines called generators. These produce electricity. Huge quantities of smoke, ash and gas are given off as the fuel burns. The fumes billow out from factory chimneys to pollute the air.

Hidden drawbacks

As well as causing pollution, using fossil fuels has other disadvantages. When these fuels are burned, they give off gases that are changing the weather and making it warmer. Fossil fuels are also being used up fast and may soon run out.

Burning fossil fuels releases carbon dioxide gas that builds up in the atmosphere. This gas traps the Sun's heat in the air, which is making Earth warmer. This process is called global warming. It is changing the world's weather, making some places wetter and others much drier.

◀ As the weather gets warmer, water in the seas will expand. As a result, over vast areas of ocean the water level could rise. This may flood coasts and islands such as the Maldives in the Indian Ocean, shown here.

Fossil fuels are called non-renewable energy resources because, once used, they are gone forever. New sources of fossil fuels are becoming harder to find as old ones run out. Experts think that the world's oil and gas stocks will only last another 70 years. Coal will last longer but will still run out in a few hundred years.

◀ *Middle Eastern countries are home to the world's largest oil fields. This is an oil refinery in Dubai in the Middle East.*

LOOK CLOSER

Burning fossil fuels releases not only carbon dioxide but also other gases, including sulphur dioxide and nitrogen oxides. When these mix with water vapour in the air, they form a weak acid, which then falls as acid rain. Acid rain kills trees, such as these firs in Poland, and poisons wildlife.

Wasting energy

The world's precious fuel stocks are not being used up by all countries equally. People in richer, industrialised countries use far more energy every day than people in poorer parts of the world.

In industrialised regions, such as Europe, North America and Japan, huge amounts of energy are used to make life easy and comfortable. Cars, computers and other machines all gobble up energy. Most of the world's coal, oil and gas stocks are found in, or transported to, industrialised regions. Dominating these natural resources have made industrialised countries richer and more powerful.

▼ Kitchens in richer countries are full of machines such as cookers, microwaves, fridges and washing machines that use large amounts of electricity.

People in poorer countries, such as in Africa, have very few machines that use up energy. People cook on open fires or simple stoves fuelled by wood or animal dung.

In poorer parts of the world, such as Africa, South America and China, people use far less energy daily. The populations of many countries there are growing quickly. These places are also becoming more industrialised, because everyone wants the machines that make life easy.

CLOSE TO HOME

One-fifth of the world's precious fuel is used by vehicles. In rich countries, most homes have at least one car. The number of cars on the road also leads to traffic jams, which are a huge waste of energy. Keep a record of all the journeys you make in a week. Are all your car journeys really necessary?

Nuclear power

W ith stocks of fossil fuels running low, we need to turn to other ways of generating energy. Nuclear power is one possibility, but it also has its disadvantages.

Nuclear energy uses a rare metal, called uranium, as fuel. Atoms (tiny particles) of uranium are split to release heat, which can be used to make electricity. Uranium is radioactive, which means it gives out harmful rays of energy. As a result, the raw uranium has to be mined and transported very carefully.

▼ *Uranium mines damage the landscape and create spoil heaps that poison local anima and plants. Nothing ca live around the mine fo a very long time.*

Nuclear energy is generated in special power stations. The fuel is used to create steam that powers a generator. Generating electricity in this way does not release the same harmful gases as fossil fuels, but it does produce deadly radioactive waste. Nuclear waste is very difficult to get rid of safely. It remains poisonous for thousands of years.

Nuclear power stations contain many safety features that make handling the fuel safer, but accidents have still happened.

LOOK CLOSER

In 1986, a nuclear power station at Chernobyl, Russia, exploded and caught fire. A huge cloud of radioactive gas escaped into the air and drifted for thousands of kilometres. People, animals and plants over a huge area were poisoned, and some people even died.

Water as energy

Fossil fuels and nuclear energy have disadvantages because they damage nature. Luckily, other forms of energy exist that cause far less pollution. These use natural forces such as wind, flowing water and sunlight. They are called renewable energy resources.

◄ *This old water mill in Bayeux, France, still works today. Humans have been usir fast-flowing water to make energy since Roman times.*

Hydroelectric power (HEP) is energy generated from flowing water. Water energy was used hundreds of years ago to turn water wheel that ground grain into flour to make bread. Generating energy from flowing water does not pollute the atmosphere or produce deadly radioactive gas, so it is much safer to use.

Hydroelectric energy is 'clean' because it produces no waste or pollution. However, it does have some drawbacks. Hydroelectricity is only available in places where there is plenty of fast-flowing water – mainly mountainous areas. The dams across rivers also sometimes take away vital water sources from local people.

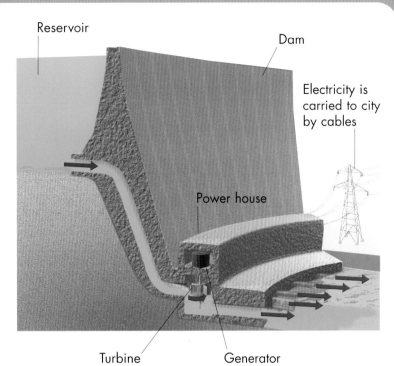

Reservoir

Dam

Electricity is carried to city by cables

Power house

Turbine

Generator

▲ *Hydroelectric plants are usually built on swift-moving rivers in hilly regions. The water flowing downhill passes through turbines in a power house. The turbines spin to turn generators that produce electricity.*

LOOK CLOSER

When a hydroelectric plant is built, the river is dammed just above it. Water builds up behind the dam to create a huge lake called a reservoir. The lake floods the landscape and kills local wildlife. Sometimes whole towns are destroyed by these large dams, and people have to leave their homes.

Weather as energy

Solar, wind and tidal power are all types of renewable energy resources. They will last as long as the Sun rises, breezes blow and tides flow. They don't pollute nature, but the machinery needed is quite expensive and doesn't always work very well.

▶ Solar furnaces like this one in Israel use mirrors to focus the Sun's rays to generate electricity.

Solar power uses energy from the Sun to heat water or generate electricity. Solar panels on a roof trap sunlight and can supply much of a family's energy needs. However, the panels are quite expensive to buy. Also, solar energy is best collected when the Sun is shining, so solar panels only work well in a sunny climate.

Tidal power stations built on river estuaries make use of the power of moving water as the tides flow in and out each day. This station is built on the River Rance in northern France. To generate electricity in this way, a structure called a barrage has to be built right across the estuary, but this can harm local wildlife.

On breezy hilltops, wind energy can be used to turn the blades of machines called turbines, which generate electricity. However, wind farms take up quite a lot of space and only work well when strong winds blow. Some people that live near wind farms also complain that the spinning turbines make too much noise.

▼ A modern wind farm consists of many turbines that turn as the wind blows.

Using rocks and waste

Energy can also be generated by burning rubbish or crop waste and even by using heat from rocks lying under the ground. These energy sources will not run out, but they are not always reliable, convenient or even clean to use.

▼ *This geothermal power station in Iceland generates large amounts of electricity.*

Geothermal energy uses heat from inside Earth to generate electricity. Water pumped underground is heated by hot rocks there to make steam. Geothermal energy can only be used in countries where the hot rocks lie fairly near the surface, such as in Iceland and New Zealand.

◄ In poorer parts of the world, animal dung is dried and then burned as fuel. However, burning dung releases carbon dioxide, which adds to the effects of global warming.

...iomass energy is made from burning crop waste such as straw or wood from trees that are especially grown for this purpose. However, burning these fuels releases the same pollution as burning fossil fuels. Every kind of renewable energy resource has drawbacks as well as advantages. The answer is to use several different energy resources, not just one.

CLOSE TO HOME

In rich countries, every household produces a lot of rubbish every week. Most of this waste is buried, but it can also be burned in incinerators to make electricity. However, the incinerators give off poisonous fumes. Getting rid of waste is a problem. The answer is to try to create less rubbish by recycling tins, bottles and paper, as these boys are doing.

Solving the crisis

Renewable energy provides part of the answer to the energy crisis, but not the whole solution. Around the world, but especially in rich countries, everyone needs to start using energy more carefully. Governments can lead the way.

At present, most energy used in rich countries is non-renewable. Clean, renewable energy resources will become the fuel of the future as fossil fuels run out. Governments can help by paying for research to develop these new energy sources. Clean energy is expensive at the moment, but it will become cheaper as it is used more.

▼ Delegates at the Earth Summit in South Africa in 2002 discuss ways to reduce the pollution caused by burning fossil fuels.

Nations Unies
SOMMET MONDIA

LOOK CLOSER

Radios provide vital news and information, but most run on electricity or on batteries that cause pollution when they are thrown away. Recently, an inventor named Trevor Baylis designed the clockwork radio, which is powered by a spring wound by hand. Now these energy-saving radios are sold around the world.

▲ Cars and other vehicles have been built that run on fuels that cause less pollution than petrol. This car runs on a solar-powered battery, which is being recharged here.

Since the 1990s, representatives from countries around the world have met at conferences called Earth Summits to try to solve the energy crisis and clean up pollution. Back at home, governments can encourage companies that make energy savings and fine those that waste energy. They can also pay for research into new energy-saving devices such as the clockwork radio.

How can we help?

Everyone can help to ease the energy crisis by using energy more carefully. At home and at school we can all start by switching off lights and machines such as computers when they are not needed. Your family can also save energy by using the car less frequently.

In many households, more energy is used on heating than by all the other machines put together. Homes that are properly insulated stay warmer and so use less fuel. Find out if your loft is insulated with glass fibre. Draughty windows can be sealed or double-glazed. In cold weather you can save energy by putting on extra clothing instead of turning the heating up.

◀ Glass from bottles you return to the bottle bank is melted down and used to make more bottles. This saves energy used to make new glass.

Vehicles use huge amounts of fuel and cause pollution. Cycling, walking, sharing cars and using public transport all save energy and create less pollution. Ask your parents if you can get to school in one of these ways.

Almost everything we buy in supermarkets these days is packaged in tins, bottles or plastic wrappers. All this packaging takes energy to make and then just gets thrown away. Save energy by asking your parents to buy products that use less packaging. Bottles, cans and wrappers should be recycled and used again.

Cycling to school is great way to exercise s well as save energy.

On sunny or windy ays, wet clothes can e hung on the line utside instead of using e tumble dryer.

Energy projects

Find out more about the energy you use at home and at school by keeping an energy diary. Your class could launch a campaign to save energy at school.

ENERGY WATCH

The amount of energy we use in homes and schools is shown on meters. Ask an adult to show you how to read the gas and electricity meter. Then watch these meters whizzing around as different machines are used.

Write down all the ways you've used energy since you got up this morning. The hot water you washed in used energy – so did the kettle or toaster used to make your breakfast. All the food you eat gives you energy, but it also takes energy to make. Then there was the energy you used to get to school.

▲ *Meters are usually found in cupboards or under the stairs. Write down the numbers shown on the meter and then compare them an hour or a day later.*

ENERGY AT SCHOOL

Make a list of all the machines that use energy at school. Don't forget the lights and heating! Does your school waste energy? Is the heating ever turned up high and windows and doors left open? Are machines left running? Are paper and other materials wasted? Remember: they all took energy to make.

Ask your teacher if your class can start a campaign to save energy. The money saved could be spent on a school trip or given to your favourite charity.

CAMPAIGN GROUPS

Friends of the Earth
26–28 Underwood Street
London N1 7JQ
Website: www.foe.co.uk

Greenpeace
Canonbury Villas
London N1 2PN
Website: www.greenpeace.org

ENERGY WEBSITES

UK Centre for Research, Education and Training in Energy: www.create.org.uk

New Scientist: www.newscientist.com

US Department of Energy information sites for kids: www.eia.doe.gov/kids

www.eren.doe.gov/energysmartschools/index.html

More energy information sites: www.kidsandtechnology.org

www.energyquest.ca.gov/index.html

◀ *Your class could set up a recycling project. Drinks cans, bottles, packaging and paper can all be recycled.*

Energy factfile

• Coal is formed from forests that grew about 300 million years ago. If you look closely at a lump of coal, you can sometimes see the fossilised remains of ferns and other plants.

• Oil, sometimes called 'black gold', is the main fossil fuel today. The companies that mine and process crude oil are some of the biggest businesses in the world.

• People in rich countries, such as the United States and Great Britain, use 1000 times more energy every day than people in poor countries.

• In 1989, the oil tanker *Exxon Valdez* hit a rock off the coast of Alaska and spilled crude oil over an area of 2600 square km. Millions of sea creatures died. In terms of damage to the environment, it was the worst oil disaster in history.

• A new dam project under way in China, called the Three Gorges Project, will flood a huge area and destroy the homes of up to two million people. It is one of the largest dam projects ever to be built.

• Almost all homes in Iceland are heated by geothermal energy.

Glossary

Acid rain
Rain that is polluted by fumes from vehicle exhausts and power stations.

Crude oil
Oil that is in its natural state and has not been changed in any way.

Fossil fuel
Coal, oil, gas and other fuels formed from the fossilised remains of plants and animals that lived millions of years ago.

Fuel
Any material that can be burned to release energy, including wood, coal, oil and gas.

Generator
A machine that produces electricity.

Global warming
A warming of the world's weather, caused by the increase of gases in the air that trap the Sun's heat. These gases, including carbon dioxide, are given off when fossil fuels are burned.

Industrialised country
A country with many factories, which makes most of its money through its industries.

Insulated
Kept warm by a material that prevents heat from escaping.

Non-renewable energy
Energy that comes from sources that will eventually run out, especially oil and gas but also coal.

Refinery
A factory where crude oil from the ground is processed to make fuels such as petrol and diesel.

Renewable energy
Energy that comes from sources that will not run out, such as the Sun, wind and tides.

Smog
Air that is polluted by smoke and gas from industry and vehicles.

Spoil heap
A pile of waste rock and earth left over from mining activities.

Turbine
A machine powered by steam, gas, wind or water to generate electricity.

Index